• • •

EARLY BIRD EXECUTIVES PRESENTS...
YOUR FUTURE STARTS NOW!

* * *

EARLY BIRD EXECUTIVES PRESENTS...
YOUR FUTURE STARTS NOW!

Shannon L. Baxa, MS, RHIA, PMP

ISBN-13: 9781517690168
ISBN-10: 1517690161

DEDICATION

To my parents—thank you for giving me this life to live. Thank you for always encouraging me to give my ALL...always.

To my husband—thank you for seeing so much more in me than I ever have. Without you, I would be doing said initial desired profession, which will remain nameless.

To all friends, family, educators, peers, mentors, and society—thank you for supporting me in all the ways you have. I owe you much appreciation for the help in shaping my life. I will forever be grateful to those that take a chance on me and have served as strong mentors in my career.

Last, to my children—be who you want to be, do what you want to do, but promise me one thing: be the best you can be at what you are doing. Never give up, and always remember that you are making an impact unknown to you now. I love you. May you always feel and truly know the love I have for you.

SLB

CONTENTS

PREFACE

★ ★ ★ ★ ★

What is that famous saying—everyone gets their start somewhere? Well, what if you are like many young people who are willing to give what it takes to fast-track up the career ladder, but you just need a little direction? Perhaps you want to see yourself achieving greater successes sooner rather than later, but you are not sure how to attain that goal or even how to start.

Perhaps you find yourself at a crossroads: continue your education or hit the market as a desirable hire. Which should you choose and why? Or maybe you are a parent who has great dreams for your child. Do you really know how to foster development and growth in all the best ways?

Well, if you have ever wondered how to accelerate your earning potential and career possibilities at a rapid rate, this series is for you! At times, this series will inspire you, make you laugh, and even make you doubt yourself. However, it will show you that you have tremendous confidence in your skills and abilities and will ultimately motivate you to take hold of your potential *NOW.*

Becoming successful is not an overnight process. However, by taking slow, steady, and gradual steps toward success, you can create strong building blocks to high career achievement. The goal of this series is to empower, enable, and encourage all young adults to see that they are truly capable of building the bridge to success. Happy reading!

# INTRODUCTION

Chapter 1

* * *

WELL, HELLO!

So there you sit, book in hand. Why the hell are you here? Did you pick this book up by accident? Did your friend have it sitting on the coffee table to use as a coaster? Well, I certainly hope your answer to both of those questions is NO! I hope you chose to grab this book to help you understand the ins and outs of making a huge impact in the corporate world. Perhaps you don't know what you want to do when you "grow up," but you *do* know that you want to be successful. Suc-cess-ful. What is success?

Success is measured in so many different ways. There are small achievements and large wins. Some success is instant, but most often, success is accomplished by making a strategic plan and following through on that plan. What if I were to tell you that you could find yourself in a position that allows you to make an excellent salary yet is also just the first step on your journey? What if I told you that you could obtain a position that will slingshot you into higher-level leadership roles within a short time? Sound too good to be true? Well…maybe. It isn't easy, but let's talk about strategy.

For me, strategy is something I had deeply ingrained within, but it did take a little coaxing to bring it forward. Before I talk about where I am today, I'd like to take you back to where my journey began. I was born to very hardworking blue-collar parents in a small town (er…OK, I guess you would actually call it a village or, more accurately, a speck on a map) of fewer than two hundred people. My parents wanted me to be happy in life and therefore were not pushy in terms of attending college, learning a trade or really any other dream I wanted to pursue. They had a pure and simple desire to see me pursue happiness in whatever way I desired. Of course my parents would have loved it if I had gone to college, but they did not make a huge effort to encourage higher education. After all, my father had held the same heavy-equipment operator job since he graduated from high school, and my mother did not graduate from high school. They had a perfect life with NO college. So, for them, college was not seen as necessary. My parents are extremely successful, happy and incredibly in love. They are the epitome of sincerely genuine GOOD people.

Heck, if there wasn't anyone demanding that I go to college, should I make the effort to do so? My initial approach was very half-assed. Yep, I registered for classes at the local community college. Did I want to go? Nope, not really. Did I do very well in my courses? Yeah, the ones that I actually attended and did not drop. Let's just say that I dicked around for a year or so. I wasted a bunch of money on courses that I did not care about or make much of an effort to complete.

I guess my story could have ended there. I could have just said screw it and called my college career complete. I likely would have ended up as a housewife or doing some menial job. I remember telling my boyfriend at the time (the same dude who would later become my amazing husband) that I was going to get a degree in tourism and travel. I boasted that I would love to get a position as a travel agent. He looked at me like I was crazy. I did not get it at the time, but my husband truly saw the potential that I was about to so nonchalantly discard. Listen, there is nothing wrong with a career as a travel agent, but if you think about it, the boom of the Internet pretty much demolished the need for travel agents, and my husband foresaw that happening.

I remember thinking, *Well, then...hmm. Shit. I guess he is right.* This was when I started to exploit the best thing that had ever happened to me career-wise. You see, because I was just strolling around taking classes, I needed some money. I found a J-O-B at a local hospital as a medical records file clerk. *Bleh. Medical records? Filing?* It sounded pretty boring to me. Well, wouldn't you know it, that position opened up some pretty progressive thoughts in my head.

I worked afternoons at the hospital. My days consisted of filing records and assembling records—one after another, the never-ending supply of medical records. Boringggg. Well, I did start to pay attention to the management team in my department. The leaders were very amazing and intelligent women with great acuity for managing people. Sure, the department had its ups and downs, but I truly became like a fly on the wall. I started asking the leaders questions about the field of medical records. *Where did you get your degree? Wait, really? You can obtain a bachelor's degree in medical records? Huh, pretty interesting.*

As I learned more, I became more and more intrigued. I also became more and more aware of the leadership's decisions—and lack thereof. I kept thinking things like, *Wait, why can't this be done this way?* Or, *Wow, I can't believe they are making us do it this way when it makes much more sense to do it that way.* There was also a whole lot of; *I think if we did this, we could see a vast improvement of that. I bet they are going to change it. Crickets. Nope. They aren't seeing it. Hello? How about we do it this way?*

Eventually, management took notice: "Oh, yes, you are right, Shannon—that would be much more effective." *Shit*, they must have thought. *This eighteen-year-old "kid" is actually bringing a lot of great suggestions. You know what? We think she can take on more tasks. Let's promote her. Promote me? Well, heck, I'll take it.* In fact, that promotion progression happened a few more times. *Wow. I kind of like this. More money, more responsibilities—this is working out nicely.* From that point on, I was slightly addicted to medical records. Yes, I realize that I am a big nerd!

I remember setting forth a path in my head. I remember thinking; *I bet I can be a leader in a department someday.* With that vision, I took the next leap that would cement my career path. I first brought the discussion up with my boyfriend. I remember exactly where we were—a Taco Bell parking lot. I dropped the bomb on him, and I am sure he was secretly smiling from the inside out.

I looked at him and said, "I want to go to Illinois State University and get a bachelor's degree in health information management." (*Health information management* is a fancy progressive term for what you all traditionally know as medical records.) I said it and then sat back and waited for his response, knowing that it meant that I would be moving away to attend that university.

Without hesitation, he said, "Awesome, I will totally support you!"

What a relief!

My next stop was to talk to my parents. The response was not as lovely. I laid it out to them, and the first response was, "Why? Why do you want to go do that?"

Well, hmm. It was not the response I was hoping for. Could I have crumpled up my dreams because they did not care and actually thought I was slightly crazy for wanting to do that? Yes, I could have, but I did not. I knew that the educational piece was going to be KEY for me to take my career to the next level. Despite the lack of understanding regarding higher education,

I owe much of my success to my parents and family (grandparents, brother, aunts, uncles, cousins, etc.). They have truly loved, nurtured and cared about me from day one. They all took so much time and effort to ensure that I had a terrific set of morals, manners and sense of self. It is a great feeling to look back on your roots and to honestly know that you had a support system that was "all in" on you as a person. I believe each of these foundational components helped to shape me into a prime candidate for both personal and professional success.

My educational story has a very happy ending. I did go on to get that bachelor's degree in health information management. None of my family really noticed. I did not go through the graduation ceremony because I knew they probably would have been resistant to attending it—not because they didn't love me, but because they didn't understand the significance. I went on to obtain a master's degree in project management. Same thing—my family was unimpressed, but my husband (transformed from previously indicated boyfriend) was over-the-top ecstatic for me. He was so proud that I took the next step in my education. That made me feel great!

I may have stumbled a little bit out of the gate, but I chalked up the lack of enthusiasm from family as resulting from their lack of understanding of the process. And that is OK! The most important thing to remember is that you will ultimately be responsible for your choices. Before you decide if the resistance or lack of support you feel is acceptable, think about your end goal. How will moving forward versus stalling and even completely stopping help or hinder your ability to achieve your goal? Luckily, I knew that the degree was like the keys to the car for me.

One successful trait that all good leaders need to have is the ability to properly evaluate the skill sets of their employees. While this sounds simple in nature, it certainly can take time and skill. Some of the evaluation process can come through tactical review, while others may take extensive time and review through scenarios.

Jumping into the driver's seat is a goal that many young professionals may have. There are many factors to consider before taking the keys such as the following:

1. What makes you a great leader?
2. How can you help this team take their operations to the next level?
3. How will you treat your most valuable asset—your people?
4. What workflow processes should be evaluated first?
5. Do you know the best way to present all types of news— the good, the bad, and the very ugly—to your staff?
6. Are you familiar with how to access all of the resources you may need to excel in your role?
7. Who can you reach out to for assistance if you and/or your team become stalled?
8. What is a realistic time frame to become fully on board as the new leader?

9. Once you are on board, how can you best fast-track to success?
10. How do you plan to maintain and foster continued growth and progress?

Continuously reviewing your ability to properly drive the car is an excellent exercise to perform. When we learn to be very introspective, we can easily exploit our weakness and enhance our strengths. I once saw the most wonderful little quote box on social media.

Three Simple Rules in Life—Author Unknown

* If you do not GO after what you want, you'll never have it.
* If you do not ASK, the answer will always be NO.
* If you do not step forward, you'll always be in the same place.

I honestly could not agree more with each of those three lines. If you equate them to the topic of career development, I think there are some great takeaways! If you do not pursue a progressive career path, you will never have it. Likewise on a smaller scale, if you do not pursue a position because you do not think you are qualified for it, that position will never be yours. I can relate to that because I have doubted myself a few times and have shied away from positions due to fear of rejection. This really is not a good mentality to have. Who cares if you get rejected? Who the hell cares if you go all the way through the interview process and they say NO—we selected another candidate!?!?! At the absolute very least, you learned a ton through the interview process and will be stronger due to that exposure.

If you do not ask, the answer will always be *NO*. This one is so true in profession and life in general. I think this is very important because if you do not bring your thoughts and ideas to the table, they will never blossom into reality. If you do not ask about taking that course Human Resources promoted a few times as a potential opportunity for some colleagues, you, my friend, will not be taking the course and someone else will! The bottom line here is that you should *NEVER EVER* be too afraid to ask or bring your ideas to the stage—you are valued, and you want to grow! Ask away!

If you do not step forward, you will always be in the same place. This particular statement is so very true when it comes to career-path management. Advancing your career is all about taking the right steps at the right time for the right opportunity. This means that moving forward is really the best way to move. The material ahead features a nine-step guide that you can focus your energy on to drive toward career success. This strategic guide is very helpful in developing framework for accelerating your goals. Let's take a look at the nine components that define your framework for success. These phases are expressed as whole chapters in this book.

The goal is to progress through each step in order, but there may be times that you will need to return to visit a previous step to make a revision or enhancement—and that's OK. Each step in this guide is very important to the life cycle of career planning. Initially, you should create a baseline approach by completing each step of the guide. However, you will likely spend time revising, enhancing, and adding by visiting these steps several times. This is typically necessary as situations evolve, goal planning changes, or we begin to better fine-tune our desire for success as our instincts lead us in a different direction. Truly following your gut instinct is something to build on. Speaking of building—where is the best place to build? The ground, of course!

 DESIGN

Chapter 2

• • •

THE STARTING GROUND

Oh, I remember it so very well! Sitting in "that seat" for the first time can be intimidating and very scary. Taking your place at the desk as a brand-new manager or director is an eye-opening experience! It also calls for some self-affirmation: *Yes, I indeed belong over on this side of the desk as your leader, Suzy Staffmember. I will not let you know that I am scared shitless and that you might not know it yet, but I will slowly start to earn your trust…starting today.*

Consider this situation from the perspective of a twenty-three-year-old "kid" just out of college, meeting with her sixty-something decades-tenured employee. Yep, you guessed it—a tad bit awkward! I was extremely fortunate to have been hired into the role by a leader who will truly forever impact my career. Without her taking a chance and trusting me to manage a department she ultimately was responsible for, I often wonder where I would be today.

Do not forget to take time to catalogue people that completely enhance your career ladder. I affectionately term these people as "super mentors" as they are professionals that will always be etched into your brain. These are the people that matter more to you than you know at times. They are often incredible advocates and typically are your biggest professional cheerleaders. Think of these people as resources that you can reach out to for advice, motivation and event to provide reference of your abilities. My super mentor continues to enhance my career ladder today and provides amazing motivation to help push me to further. I feel unbelievably blessed to have found her.

My first day on the job in my first leadership role of operations manager was very interesting. I began my day by meeting one-on-one with each of my ten staff members. The very first staff member was in her sixties and had been working in the department for decades. Hell, I was young enough to be her granddaughter, and I was *HER* new boss. Typically, a leader does not instantly gain the respect of his or her employees—respect is earned and not automatically given.

In this scenario, the respect that I wanted was not going to fall into my lap quickly by any means. If you think about it, why would it? Why would this woman who was in her forties when I was born—let me repeat that...she was forty-something *WHEN I WAS BORN*—instantly trust me as her leader? By its nature, being young and in a professional role definitely has its downfalls. Whereas age discrimination is not tolerated, there seems to be an unsaid level of skepticism when a wide age gap exists between colleagues, reporting staff, consultants…(insert any type of role you would like here).

Well, then, Suzy Staffmember, it is very nice to meet you! I would like to start understanding some processes and baseline information and get right to work in my new role.

Whoa, hold on, Ms. You-Certainly-Look-Young! I want to be the first to tell you all about things that have been discussed, but will NEVER work in this department.

Oh, Suzy Staffmember, let me count the ways I loathe pessimism!

Consider this thought for a moment: there is something to be gained, lost, and most definitely embraced through various decades of our lives. Typically, from the age of ten through twenty, it is all about education and socialization. Adolescents, teens, and young adults are focused on exploring the world around them. During this time, development and enhancement of many inborn characteristics are augmented through social interactions and family mentoring. There are often many peaks and valleys to the roller coaster that is life during this period. There is often much heartache realized to a certain extent and the typical main focus placed upon younger adults is centered on ensuring strong fundamental development.

This youth time frame is vital for later stages in life as many "lessons" taught here will be brought forward in blatant and discrete capacities. Concepts such as self-esteem, social acceptance, and overcoming stressful situations really assist in developing a child into a young adult. During this time, young adults are faced with completing school, determining who their friends and enemies are, along with so much focus on life itself. This time frame can be volatile and fraught with flashes of brilliance and stupidity.

Keeping young adults on a positive healthy track is something that most parents want to see their child achieve. Unfortunately, this period is not without tears, agony, bliss, and other extreme emotions (sometimes all of those feelings in one day!) Parents, family, and friends are the foundation for helping young adults grow into the beginnings of a successful professional. In many instances, zero or minimal money is earned during this time; however, countless skills are learned and often fine-tuned—even if that tuning is occurring silently!

The next decade, ages twenty through thirty, is all about discovery and career-plan creation. Many individuals may find this as a launching point to their careers and see this blastoff as the start of their increased money-making year. It is twenty through thirty where intensive planning and goal-setting help to propel future success. While we enter this decade possibly not knowing where our paths will take us, we should be exiting with a strong plan that will catapult us into our money-making years of our thirties.

Besides younger professionals needing to understand the level of strategic planning that is required to set goals, family members or friends supporting this drive also need to under-stand the focus that is required within this decade. This decade again will be full of ups and downs—possibly family changes, lifestyle changes, moving residences, love-life changes, possibly marriage, possibly divorce, and any other life-altering change could happen during this period. Professional success does not happen by chance. Successful performance and drive happen when individuals are goal-oriented and have a strategic plan.

It is also important to have a good understanding of the next level of progression. You will not know your path for certain; however, during this decade you should be laser-focused on your career-ladder development. The best laid plans are not always the way life goes. This is true especially during the beginning decades of life. Possessing flexibility to alter the course when you know something is not going the way you planned is sign of a strong individual. While it may be devastating at the time, and you may feel weak from different levels of failure, this action may turn out to be a blessing in disguise or possibly a fork in the road for other successes and wins.

It's quite possible that a failed attempt at one thing may result in a positive path indicator for a door you never even imagined may open. When I started my roots as a medical records file clerk, I thought I was walking into a job that would provide me with a little bit of cash to get by on my own. I had no clue that the opportunity would result in such a snowball of actions that would lead to my ultimate passion for the profession that I am in today. Do not always assume that your situation is static and cannot grow into something more.

We have heard of great professionals, musicians, artists, and so forth, being discovered by someone at the most mundane time—for example, a waitress who serves lunch to a record executive. Possibly some small talk leads to another conversation about a potential opportunity. Random interactions may result in dead ends left and right, but don't be afraid to take a risk if your gut is telling you that the situation is worthy of your attention. Conversely, not all situations are worthy of your attention! There are people and situations that turn out to be scams or schemes for money or prey on those looking for an opportunity.

While I tend to believe that everything happens for a reason, do not turn your nose up to the simple notion of *LUCK*. If you find yourself in a situation that cannot be explained other than the fact that you were in the right place at the right time, it is quite OK to be grateful for your bounty. Likewise, you may have doors slammed in your face from time to time. You may job hunt for twenty-four months straight before you find an opportunity or convince someone to give you that chance. Do not get discouraged! I understand it's much easier said than done. Discouragement can really hinder one's ability to foresee or foreshadow potential opportunities.

A positive attitude and one that does not become easily rattled often accompanies a person who is more prone to benefit from decisions and situations. If you have a negative attitude and are constantly thinking that nothing good will ever happen to you, you may completely ignore an opportunity that is staring back at you. The twenty-through-thirty years may be skewed or altered by your desire for socialization with friends, family dynamics, or even a love relationship. Finding a love interest, partner, or a solid friendship can mean the difference in your career acceleration in a positive or negative way.

If you find yourself in a negative relationship with a person who is putting you down and not believing in your potential, that person could set your career and your success back years. If you find someone who understands you, supports you, and is willing to give you the benefit of the doubt if you wish to take a risk, hold on to that person. That person is letting and helping you steer your career path in a positive direction.

I know I spoke about my husband a few times in this book, and to me, he could have easily help turn my path the other way had he not been supportive. What I mean by this is, at times I was fragile and impressionable. I mentioned that I was not taking my classes seriously and dropped a bunch of them. He could have easily just stated that I was never going to be able to do it. I hate to admit it, but that might have been enough negativity to make me snap. However, because he was raised with such strong morals within such a supportive family structure, he found it within himself to build me up and make me feel that I was somewhat invincible, maybe even a bit stronger than I really was. He helped me maintain my composure when I thought my world was falling. That's the type of person you want in your life, be it a mentor, a teacher, a friend, a coworker, or anyone positive in your life.

I recently talked to one of my students who really wanted to quit school. She found it overwhelming to maintain her studies along with working, but she really wanted to see the program through. She knew the benefits of the academic program and really had the desire to move forward, but she felt completely overwhelmed. I was very happy that she reached out to me. I talked her through the path to progress forward and get back on track. She referenced a coworker who had been her biggest cheerleader and support system. She mentioned the coworker was quite a bit younger than she was because this was her attempt to return to school for a new career path. I thought that story was excellent because a coworker, maybe somebody she least suspected, was performing a duty of being a support person for this student.

If you find yourself in a negative situation and are feeling trapped with a lover or friend, it is vital that you begin to focus on yourself and your future. Most times, people who are disruptive to us are selfish, and they do not care about our future well-being; they care mostly about how you are impacting them today. They may say negative things to you because they are fearful that they could lose you, and they may also be intimidated that you were taking steps to better yourself. Sometimes, people are manipulative. They know exactly what they are doing, and they are literally trying to remove you from your path.

It is so important that you begin to understand why certain people are treating you in either a positive or negative way. Again, easier said than done as our emotions can be clouded by other factors, but this knowledge component is extremely important. I think it is a good practice to center on building others up so that they may advance along the career-ladder process. This is really important as it helps us identify where we see ourselves going. It is the goal that in our twenties and thirties we see progression climb the career ladder to a pretty decent rate. Creation of the ladder framework should be completed or in full force by the middle to early part of this decade. The earlier the career-path goal is defined, the stronger the resiliency and faster the career-path growth can occur. It doesn't matter when you start as long as you actually do it.

A little bit ago, I mentioned the notion of "money-making years" as a segue into a quick little story. My husband and I had our first home years ago, which was a townhome. We purchased a hot tub for our lower basement area. We had no kids, so it was our project to do together—just him and I! Our goal in creating a bit of a sanctuary was that it would be a little place to kind of get away, and it turned out to be a really nice area. However, the hot tub became a little bit of a pain in the ass to maintain, and we decided that we wanted to move on from the room.

We placed an ad on an Internet classified site that everyone knows—the one that starts with a *C*. It is kind of funny that you meet people in the weirdest places at the weirdest times, and I still firmly believe that things happen for a definite reason. In this situation, we happened to meet a very intriguing later middle-aged couple who came to our house to look at the hot tub and determine if they wanted to purchase it. My husband likes to talk, and well, I guess I do, too! We started talking with this couple and something was said about our careers at the time. The gentleman was very impressed with what we had accomplished to date and told us to carry those goals and skills into our money-making years.

My husband and I never really heard of that terminology, and we really weren't sure what exactly he meant. However, he went on to elaborate a little further. He said that he enjoyed a very successful career and also had a family to celebrate life with. He explained to us that you really begin to see and realize your hard work in your thirties. We were in our midtwenties at the time, trying to grind away and focus on building our careers and lives in general. I tend to think my husband and I both had our heads pretty straight on for the most part in our twenties. Sure, we made some mistakes, and we still make mistakes. Listening to the man talk about his family and work-life balance was awesome. The concepts he spoke about really made a lot of sense and helped us look at things a bit differently.

He talked about setting yourself up and your money-making years, which he termed as mainly peaking in your thirties and forties, so that when you are in your fifties, sixties, and so on, you are primed for a very positive retirement experience. He retired in his fifties, and he made it seem as though he had set himself up so well with his family so that he now was really living the best years of his life. Money was not a major stressor for him because he'd put so much hard work into his twenties, thirties, and forties. As we all know, learning and career paths really have no age parameters. However, I think it is safe to say that most people land their first position between ages sixteen and eighteen—sometimes later depending on school situations—and work through their sixties depending on their situation.

I honestly feel the most in tune with myself at thirty-three than I ever have. I feel completely satisfied with my life to date. Of course, I have made mistakes, yet I try to maintain a very positive outlook on what I've done to date. I think the thirties to the forties start to become more relaxed in some ways. Perhaps you got married and had kids in your twenties, have strong focus on your career in your thirties, and you are slowly becoming more settled into your routine of sorts.

Your children may be older, and your family work-life balance may be a little bit easier to determine. You may understand more about your spouse's or partner's expectations, or be used to your situation of maybe choosing not to have a partner and being single. Wherever you are in life, in my opinion, your thirties are a little bit of a breath of fresh air. That being said, from a career perspective, I think your thirties are the pedal to the ground of your career development. In your thirties, you are still continuing to grow professionally. You should be accelerating your career in your thirties; however, you may notice a slower or faster rate depending on where you took things in your twenties.

I think your thirties are great because you may have more exposure to the corporate or trade world—wherever you find yourself—and you know a little bit more of the lay of the land. You are not a wide-eyed twenty-something who has the drive and wants to take it to the next level but don't know exactly where to make each move. We will never know every right move because that's how fate works. However, in your thirties you should be more equipped to accelerate your career potential.

If you do not step forward, you will always be in the same place. This particular statement is so very true when it comes to career-path management. Advancing your career is all about taking the right steps at the right time for the right opportunity. This means that moving forward is really the best way to move. I don't know about you, but I would rather be first in a marathon than be some schmuck standing at the finish line for minutes as I get blown past. However, quite frankly, it does not matter if you find yourself in a sprint, a jog, a walk, or a simple stroll—*KEEP ON MOVING!* Speaking of moving—let's mosey on over to another type of exercise.

LAUNCH

Chapter 3

● ● ●

GETTING THERE: THE EXERCISE

There is no doubt that attaining a position with a high potential for both salary and career growth is not necessarily an easy task. It is by no means something that anyone—let alone new professionals—will just walk right into.

The process takes careful planning and strategy. I would love to be the magical author to publish a step-by-step career success manual that is a one-stop shop to follow. That "magical" book will, unfortunately, never come into existence. For obvious reasons, positions, industries, required skill sets, and other factors all greatly vary. However, you can align yourself with a fast track to success by focusing on the following five key components as the true guide to your part of the deal. Guess what? Cue the corny game-show music and announcer voice: It's time for…THE EXERCISE! Quick—say these five words out loud in your best announcer voice. Ready? GO.

1. Review
2. Define
3. Determine
4. Trial
5. Accelerate

Well, that was fun and silly. I bet those five words have never had such a snazzy introduction in their lives. I know they sound so boring, yet I hope they are also intriguing to you at this point. Let's look at what each of these means in our career context.

1. **REVIEW:** You have been taught from a very young age that you need to review the situation before moving further. This can be seen in those pesky math problems, such as, "Jane has five apples, and Billy takes one away. How many apples is Jane left with?" Well, geesh, if only you were reviewing something as simple as that! Truthfully, the reviewing stage really means that you are taking a deep, intricate look at where you are starting from. This may mean reviewing academics or your chance of success in your chosen major. If you are out of the current academic scene, reviewing may mean thinking about your current career search or even your current position.

   By breaking down the item to the lowest part possible, you can more easily assess the status of the whole.

For instance, you may review your current position with a fine-tooth comb. You discover that you enjoy your position, and you feel that you are learning from your position, but you know that you can handle so much more responsibility. These are excellent points to identify and will help you in the next phase of defining. Now, go grab a blank piece of paper, and let's see those breakdown boxes appear!

2. **DEFINE:** Great job! You have a wonderful baseline review of your current state. This sounds so simple, yet sometimes, we get so caught up in the day-to-day grind that we don't take time to stop and map out our current setting. So now that you have your breakdown boxes from the review stage, let's further define each of those puppies, along with where you want to go from here. Moving from box to box, write (1) your best thought or opinion on how the description makes you feel; (2) your thought for what will happen next with the box; and finally, (3) whether you see that box as transitioning to a new definition or new box entirely, and if the latter, what that new box is. Throw in some arrows, new shapes, or anything you feel to express your definitions of starting states to where you want to go next.

   Now, I know you are probably thinking that this exercise is a bit odd. I assure you that at the end of this mapping, you will have much more clarity into where you are today, where you want to go, and how the heck you can get there. Once you know those steps, you can go back and fill in the actions you need to take to achieve those steps. Again, we are not talking about some hard-as-hell algebraic correlation here. We are simply talking about an exercise that is somewhat boring, requires no use of technology, and is an old-fashioned pen-to-paper task. Let's continue!

3. **DETERMINE:** Well, you did it, you sumbitch. You did it—you successfully reviewed what you have right now, and then you began to define the start to a sneaky plan, or what I like to call a systematic plan, for "getting there." Now, let's next determine the actions you need to take to get there. Take a look back to your simple yet robust white piece of paper. You should see boxes that review your baseline and then some additional notations to those boxes that will kick off your review. Next, let's consider determining how to get to where you want to go.

   For example, let's assume your current job uses a sophisticated software program and that you can become certified in the use of this program, which will qualify you for a higher-grade job. In this case, you might write something like "Learn _____ software" on or near a box that highlights career progression to the next job grade.

   Or, let's say you are a junior project manager. In your career review, you indicated that you want to take the jump to be a senior project manager. If in your determining stage you drew that wonderful new box to document the promotion to a senior project manager, but you need project management certification to get to that box, go ahead and add that action of obtaining certification on or near that box.

I think you get the point here. In this step of the exercise, you are going above reviewing and defining; you are now determining your actual actions and steps to get to the next level.

4. **TRIAL:** This phase of the exercise is very important. I call this the *extreme honesty section*. Sure, you reviewed what you had. You defined the specifics of what you have and where you want to go next, and you also took the brave action of determining how to best get there. Now you move on to the trial stage. The trial stage involves thinking through what will happen if you take the actions you determined were necessary to take the next steps. You should look at this phase both humbly and confidently, both honestly and ferociously.

Now, let's go back to our example requirement of learning a software program and becoming certified in that program. What may happen in this situation? You may attempt to learn the program but fail the certification test, you may learn the program and pass the certification with flying colors, or you may not make any effort to learn the program and never get certified. Each of those trial actions is a path that you could take.

As one of my favorite old-time country music songs states, we have choices. When deciding which choice you are going to push forward with, you must learn to accept the consequences. In our example scenario, if you don't learn the software at all or if you try but fail, there is no possibility of moving your career to the next position in the progression. If you invest your time and learn the program and then pass the certification, you set yourself up as a stronger candidate for the promotion.Your actions and choices all depend on where you determine you want to go. These determinations are fluid and are expected to change several times. They will shift—sometimes growing stronger and more aggressive, and sometimes laying low and becoming less emphatic.

As a young professional, this ebb and flow will also coincide with your social-, love-, and family-life dynamics. You may have every gosh darn intention in the world to sit for that project manager certification exam. You may want to take that exam and kick its ass so bad that you cannot stand it anymore. However, you may also learn that you are expecting your first baby, you may put it off for your wedding, or a parent may become ill and your focus is needed there. And guess what? That is all OK! This is your career path to manage.

Life knows no boundaries—tragedies, stalling events, and life-changing happy events happen all the time. Do not beat yourself up if you need to change your determinations over and over. This is why flexibility in the professional area of your life is so important. I got news for ya. Yep, this exercise is awesome. The results are handy as hell, but pick that cute little paper back up one more time. That paper and the items on it do not know or care that the reason you are not pushing forward to obtain an advanced degree that you yourself have mapped out and want so much is because your brother had a severe car accident and needs your attention.

Only you know why you are straying from your plan. *OK*, you might be thinking, *what if I just start to slack a little? I know what I want and how I can get there. But, I tell ya, there are not enough hours in the day to focus on studying.* Guess what? That is OK, too! However, here is my BIG caveat: don't find yourself drowning in excuses that you tell yourself so many times that you start to believe them. Again, cut yourself some slack if your plan slips, changes, or needs to be ripped up altogether. *However,* do not allow yourself to sit stagnant without gaining the traction that a talented young professional needs to push forward. I will tell you that this almost happened to me, but I recognized it instantly and made adjustments.

Let's just say that I was working for a giant in the technology field. I worked remotely from home and conquered my daily tasks with no problem. I was constantly receiving positive reviews from management and peers. I was one who replied to e-mails instantly and never skipped a beat. To the world, I was Johnny-on-the-spot, busting my ass to provide that level of service/support. To me, though, I was bored as *HELL* toward the end! I managed my time so effectively that I was able to handle the workload of sixty-plus hours in a fraction of the time. The rest of the time I had to myself and for other tasks. Again, I overachieved for my stakeholders in a fraction of the time of a typical work week. Well, shit… that's great, right? Some cushy corporate job, pleasing everyone left and right, a valued high producer on the team who can be counted on for quick response, always exceeding goals, *and* having so much extra free time that not a day went by when I didn't find time to go outside for walks for extensive "me" time. Who wouldn't want that arrangement? Well, I can tell you who didn't want it: *ME*. Can you guess why? I was *SOOOOOO BORED*!

Sure, I had it made—all the time in the world during my day for shopping, lounging, and family commitments, and still succeeding, all while making a great salary and benefits. Well, I was bored because I was not being stimulated at all. I felt I was not growing in the direction that I wanted to grow. I likely could have easily stayed in that role for years to come, but I would not let myself. Although I did not know my potential initially (and thanks to my husband for always seeing it!), once I got a taste of where I could take my career and earning potential, I was not about to sit and be a bump on a log.

There is no damn way! If you want a mediocre career with a status quo potential, then you are not going to get much out of my books (yes, *books*—this is the first in a series). However, if you are like me and start to see top executives in their roles and think, *Why can't I do that?* then you, my friend, are exactly why Early Bird Executives was founded! Whew—well I know that was a lot of information in the trial step of our exercise, but I think it is important. The goal in the trial step is to forecast what may happen if you succeed, fail, do nothing, or take another approach.

5. **ACCELERATE:** *I wanna go fast! I wanna go fast!* I hear you, but hold up a bit, Skipper. Yes, I have been preaching moving forward throughout this book, and you will hear the term *fast-track* in many publications of this series. That is definitely the mentality that you want and need to have to grind out your place in growing your career. But when we look at accelerating here, we are focusing on a systematic way to not only speed up the process, but to also enhance the process.

It is important to set appropriate goals along the way. Not everyone can successfully hit six figures by age thirty. Others may hit six figures *WELL BEFORE* age thirty, whereas others may hit the mark later. And each of those trends is completely fine. What truly and honestly matters at the end of the day is that you took your career by the nuts and developed a custom plan—*JUST FOR YOU!* You then used that plan, tweaked it, added to it, erased from it, put thought into it while you were on the shitter, thought about it while daydreaming at the beach—whatever action you took on the plan is an action in the right direction. Getting too big too fast is almost always a recipe for concerns to come your way. When you slow it down a bit and truly identify your plan, then and only then can you see acceleration in your career and, most importantly, in your direct deposit!

Well, well, well, look what **YOU** just did. Do you know that you just put more thought, planning, effort, and focus on your career than some people put forth in decades? The notion and process of career planning really aren't things that we are taught. Hell, we don't always even get an introduction from our parents to career planning. In addition, not all employers give a shit about your career plan. In fact, many cringe when they think they have to find a replacement for you at your position level, rather than seeing benefit in an individual growing his or her potential. My husband, who is an active real-estate agent, once told me something that really stuck with me. In his line of business, it is not really about the transaction of the particular house being sold; it is, rather, the experience of the customer thinking of you for all real-estate needs in his or her life. Do yourself a favor: don't let your employer look at you as a transaction. Be your own agent who is results-focused on your entire career "life." Good news—the phone is ringing. It's for you!

EARN

Chapter 4

* * *

CONGRATS—WE WANT YOU!

You search and you search—scrolling through Internet pages, sometimes still flipping through newspaper classifieds, networking, networking, and a bit more networking. And then it happens: you find a position that fits you like a glove. You apply for the position; you send your résumé and other supporting documents in a nice and neat little package. You wait. And you wait some more. And then, OMG, the phone rings. You can't believe what you are hearing: "We want to interview you for the role of manager of operations." *Wow. Manager of damn operations! Me? Wow, is that accurate?* Yep! They confirm the date, time, and location for your interview. Shit is getting real.

You prep all you can for the interview. You study the company history, you know what every acronym listed on the company's services page stands for, and you feel like you are totally going to nail the interview. Now, what to wear? Should you go for ultra-professional, modern-chic professional, a bit more casual, or just a classic, timeless look? Well, you can't go wrong with classic, so you hit the road early to arrive with plenty of time to spare.

Waking into the interview, you feel like a champ. You freaking nailed it! Snazzy professional attire, a portfolio filled with accolades to make you blush, and a smile. You've got this. You walk your happy little ass to that chair and sit down with grace. *Phew!* You didn't anticipate being so nervous! Your heart is fluttering a bit faster, your skim is clammy, and you are glad you remembered deodorant today!

So, next you hear a stern voice mumble, "Tell me about yourself."

Really? Crap. You knew this generic shitty question would be asked. *Here we go.* You go on to talk about your experience to date, your education, what you feel you bring to the team, and where you see yourself going. You pause to see a seemingly unimpressed expression looking back at you.

Well, then. Heck, I guess I am not the one for this position. You start to finally relax because, at this point, who the hell cares how you are coming across? You certainly do not feel like you are a good candidate for this position. You start to concede mentally, and then it happens. The flat-expression, I-don't-like-what-you-are-telling-me interviewee says something that will burn in your mind forever.

He says, "You know what? I really like you. I think you might have what it takes to make a big impact here. I do have one concern," he goes on to babble. "You might be a tad bit green for this role. Tell me how you will command the respect of the more seasoned team members."

You pause. *Hmm, what is the best way to answer this one?* You decide to highlight why innovation and progressive thinking would come into play here. You go on for about three minutes, expressing that while others may have more experience than you, you are extremely committed to innovative thinking and challenging the status quo.

You tell the interviewer that you do not like to sit complacent, and acknowledge that there are always bountiful opportunities among us. You conclude your response by stating that you firmly believe that the most successful teams are made up of a diverse combination of members. You further explain how each member contributes in his or her own distinct way, and how the collective approach of various minds can help this company achieve great things right here and right now. *Phew.* You really did nail it.

You find yourself not breathing for a few seconds as the interviewer looks square into your eyes and says three magical words: "We want *YOU!*"

Hell, yeah, you are beyond excited! Now the fun and exciting process of negotiating your offer package suddenly smacks you clear across the face. *How much money will they offer me? What will my benefits look like? How many vacation days will I get?* AHHH so many questions! These are all important things that deserve consideration. Let me give you a few words of caution, however: wait for the offer! You can sit and imagine what you may be offered. There are even websites that effortlessly display ranges of salaries for positions within a geographical region. I definitely encourage you to use all resources available to narrow down what an acceptable offer might look like.

Don't forget that offers are typically negotiable. You can negotiate items such as salary, benefits, hire date, and so on if you feel that you would like to see something different. Of course, there is always risk to this action. Each person must weigh the situation, offer, and interaction to determine if asking for changes is appropriate. When anticipating an offer, you should definitely hold tight and wait on determining any dead-set parameters around your make-or-break point. Time is your best friend in these situations, and it is best to wait for the offer to arrive, determine how long until a response is required, and then plan out your course of action.

This is a recurring theme in this book, but I will say it again and with emphasis here: YOU are responsible for your career path. You make the choices based on what you truly feel is in your best interest. Do not be afraid or reluctant to seek assistance from your support system. They do not need to know any more details than you feel comfortable providing. For instance, if you truly do not feel comfortable discussing the salary component with your brother, but you really want to pick his brain on the opportunity at large, go for it! If you are confronted with the question about the salary, you can tactfully downplay the question and guide the discussion back to the topic at hand.

Time is typically of the essence once an offer has been extended. Again, be sure to fully understand expectations around a response time line as well as any other questions you may have before investing considerable time in reviewing the offer. Remember, the employer is the one hiring you, but you are also deciding if the employer is the right partner for you. You may even find yourself with multiple offers, and sorting them out can become complex. This has happened to me in the past, and I wholeheartedly recommend that you use some sort of tool—whether it be a spreadsheet, whiteboard, or scratch paper—to keep the offer components distinct.

Finally, there really is no right or wrong answer per se to an offer. In fact, there may be components of the offer that you love and others that you feel you are settling on a bit. Perhaps it is an offer for more of an entry-level positon, but you are forecasting that the opportunities within the company may be amazing and worth some time to achieve. The unfortunate part about making a decision is that you truly do not know what you do not know. You may beat this offer off the wall every which way, only to learn that, despite all of your due diligence, it was truly not the best direction to take. Guess what? That is quite OK! Most likely, you will still learn a great deal from the experience and find that it has truly set you up to be more powerful and stronger than ever. Or you could land yourself in a positon that is exactly what you thought it would be, and the match is incredibly rewarding. Either way, go forth, my friend. You have nowhere to go but up, so embrace each opportunity!

Chapter 5

FANCY FINANCIAL FOCUS!

Oh yes, the almighty dollar—it makes the world go around and also drown at times. Well, I have a bit of news for you. While money is fabulous, I truly stand by the old adage that money cannot buy happiness. However, that being said, money CAN buy a lot of *THINGS*! Zero in on that word "things"

I remember seeing a great short phrase of all the things money CAN'T buy, which includes manners, respect, honesty, integrity, loyalty, treating people the way they deserve to be treated, and so on. Those are a few of the vital traits and actions that I believe compose a positive person. Many of these traits are taught by our parents, families, and other influencing factors. They are typically ingrained from a young age, and all the money in the world will never grant integrity.

By nature, the entire goal of obtaining a degree or position that allows for advancement is the hope and desire to make either substantial money or, at the very minimum, adequate money. Unfortunately, not everyone will have this capability. It is important to understand that there are different factors that go into earning a healthy salary. Likewise, if you do not have a positive lifestyle coupled with the ability to pinpoint what makes you happy, all the money in the world will mean nothing to you if you cannot find enjoyment in your soul.

We all hear stories of the defunct athlete who had all the money in the world but lost at all and is no longer thriving as he once was. Sometimes, money can be an illusion of sorts as one may think that it will always be plentiful. If you think back to the dot-com Internet bust and then the housing bubble bursting, you will remember that so many professionals who were living the high life quickly saw their fortune go up in smoke. Likewise, we hear stories of people who recall childhoods fraught with financial struggles. Sometimes, these people have the greatest memories and corresponding excellent values. When we find this, oftentimes it is because of their parents' or other caregivers' focus on truly emphasizing the importance of being a good person. With this, any dollar amount can equal happiness. However, for a career focus, we are going to chat with an emphasis that you have a goal or desire to achieve a bigger and better financial return on your career investment.

Let's think back to the notion that we all have choices in our lives. It would be reasonable to expect that someone who has not put forth a considerable effort may not anticipate as much of a return as someone who spends thousands of dollars on education and personal growth. While there are many dynamics to define what a "considerable" amount of effort equates to, typical efforts include the time, money, and blood/sweat/tears that go into career focus.

Because this series focuses on mentoring young adults into becoming successful businesspeople, let's talk about the dynamics of salary. This is one difficult area that new professionals may find somewhat confusing. There is a fine art to determining what pay range is associated with certain positions. This could be a very tricky situation, as you want to get solid experience and allow for growth, but you also know that you need to start somewhere, even if at the bottom. In certain occasions, access to the salary range defined for a role may be possible. However, you should always do your own due diligence to understand the ceiling, floor, and average of the typical position in a similar company within your region.

The actual salary offered for any particular role is usually completely variable across organizations. A software engineer position with one company may pay $20 per hour while a different company may offer $40 per hour for a similar position. If you do not understand the typical baseline, you may sell yourself short. An additional burden that new professionals often encounter is the old question: "What is your desired salary?" or something to that effect. This becomes difficult because you don't want to be too over advantageous and price yourself out of the position.

However, on the opposite end of the spectrum, you may assume that the salary rate is much lower than it actually is, which could possibly lead to different interactions with the hiring company. Typically, many professionals leave the salary requirements section pretty vague.

There are some sectors of industry that typically pay more than others. Some positions will never achieve skyrocketing salary potential. I say this caveat as it is unrealistic for you to expect to attain a six-figure salary with certain roles, certain companies, or certain opportunities. You really need to educate yourself on the salary ceiling, which means what is the top dollar range for a typical salary in this position that you can achieve. It is also important to understand the average salary for someone within this type of role. Last, having an idea of where the salary floor is will help you know the minimum pay rate that you can expect.

This baseline salary knowledge is key to determining how you will build your career ladder. If you think you can obtain a position as a dog walker at age twenty-five and expect to use the tools and tips embedded in this book to obtain a six-figure salary, you are not setting a realistic expectation. As professionals, we need to set standards for where we are willing to see our career move toward. Now, if you say that you are going to accept an entry-level paralegal position with a very large and growing international law firm, you may have the potential to grow within that position. Again, there is no magic wand to determine what role will have the most growth potential; however, we can use the facts and our best judgment to determine most promising roles. In the example we just reviewed, there is writing on the wall to suggest that the paralegal position may be a viable position with tremendous growth potential. You have a large company that has an international footprint; they likely already employ higher level positions that can be roles that you may possibly find yourself as a viable candidate. In the dog-walker example, the ceiling of what someone may pay for dog-walking services is extremely limited, and there are no other positions to which you can be promoted.

This scenario is almost like a concept that my husband has cited before in his real-estate world. Buying the worst house in the best neighborhood is an opportunity to see a return on your investment when you sell because you chose a home that has potential for improvement to become aligned with the higher priced homes. If you were to buy the best house in the worst neighborhood, you may never see your money come back to you at all. This same thought process is in play for career choices.

If you choose an industry that has a cap on how far typical associates can grow, you need to be realistic in your expectations that you may never achieve high compensation. The ability to attain a high-paying position when the leaders in the company with much more experience are not earning a strong salary is another unrealistic expectation.

Having your eyes squarely on the prize is so damn important. If you love the field where the lower salary parameters are found, then it is fine to go for what you are passionate about. We talked about before that you really need to love what you're doing, and money does not buy happiness. If you are dead set on becoming a social worker, and you have completed research to find that even with decades of experience, the highest level of pay you can attain is XYZ and that the average salary range is well below where you desire your salary to be, then you need to set the correct expectation in your mind. However, if you love the field and want to go for it, just be sure that your expectation is not that you are going to make $300,000 a year after ten years of service. This would be a very skewed and incorrect foreshadowing because it is not realistic.

Now, people talk about general career fields and respective majors such as business. One positive of studying in a general field is that you are really leaving your doors open for quite a variety of positions across different industries. This is excellent, but the supply/demand of individuals with a business degree might be more in favor of supply. There may be five hundred people competing with you for a position that requires a bachelor's of science in business.

I will utilize my field as an example of what more of a niche or specialty concentration looks like. I have a bachelor's of science in health information management. This is basically a health-care business specialty area that focuses on revenue cycle and medical records oversight for hospitals and other health-related entities. The great thing about my position and my field is that there is a limited supply of professionals, which stems from a limited number of academic programs that grant this degree. There is also a certification component and that everyone who sits for this exam has a desire to take their potential to new heights.

This specialized degree sets myself and others apart from many other people who might want to obtain a health-care revenue-cycle position. Sure, a person with a business degree might be able to do some of the positions that someone with my degree can do. However, I set the tone for my career by choosing a specialized path because I knew there was a limited supply of workers.

There is a very good guide through the United States Department of Labor that is a career outlook guide called the *Occupational Outlook Handbook* (http://www.bls.gov/ooh/). This guide tells you plenty about all kinds of careers. It displays projected rate of growth, projected number of people needed, salary ranges, and some of the positions that have an extreme shortage.

Choosing a career that does have high ceiling for growth and accelerated salary opportunities is key. If you look through that career outlook guide and choose a position that states the average salary is $32,000 through $55,000, it is not realistic for you to expect to make six figures by the age of thirty in that industry or that role. However, if you choose an industry that is much more booming, has much greater growth, and has an average salary of $75,000 through $275,000, then you may have found an excellent candidate to determine if that field might be something you're interested in.

You should *never* base your desires and goals on salary alone. Determining your career path or industry of choice needs to be driven by factors including the desires, dreams, and hopes of your career aspirations or a combination thereof and, I repeat, *not* on salary alone.

As you can see, this is a multifaceted decision, and quite frankly, you are not making a final decision on anything; rather, you are determining where you should spend your time and investment. You should make sure your thirties and forties are filled with regular reviews of your career path and whether you want to make a move up, across, or down your plan.

UNDERSTAND

Chapter 6

• • •

AVOIDING YOUNG LEADER PITFALLS

There are hundreds of articles, books, blogs, and websites that highlight pitfalls in leadership. Depending on with whom you speak, some traits are more concerning than others. When it comes to new leaders, I think the learning curve can be quite steep, and it is good practice for professionals to understand their weaknesses. Many of you have heard of the acronym *SWOT*. This is a registry of your strengths, weaknesses, opportunities, and threats. By understanding our weaknesses, we can develop plans on how we will overcome our threats. Likewise, a catalog of our strengths can help us exploit our opportunities.

There are many well-known personality assessments that can be purchased along with business skills review tests that can really review a person's inventory of traits. I have chosen five of what I consider to be the biggest pitfalls new leaders may encounter. By understanding that these risks are present, new professionals will arm themselves with the tools to avoid pitfalls.

48

Newbie Leader Pitfall #1: Sitting in Silence

Overview: By being "silent," a leader is not effectively communicating with his or her team. Having good communication skills is one of the most important traits a leader can have. In a professional sense, sitting in silence entails not giving feedback. To foster growth and a positive work experience, employees need and desire both positive and constructive feedback. It is a main focus of a leader to provide feedback as well as detailed process information so that the employee totally understands how well they are achieving the tasks at hand. Another example of sitting in silence is when leaders to not update their teams on upcoming events, company changes, and so forth. When the lack of relaying information occurs, leaders run the risk of staff members learning about something through outside sources. This can result in misinformation or resentment because staff members feel as though they are an afterthought.

Risk: Lack of communication can be a leader's biggest error. When staff members begin to feel as if they are not important, they quickly become disengaged. When staff members are disengaged, there is a risk of loss of respect for their leader, development of resentment for their position, and most importantly, staff members may revolt independently or as a group, which can result in loss of productivity or overall team momentum.

Overcoming: Leaders who have engaged employees who truly feel valued will perform much better than angry employees. I do not feel that it is even possible for new leaders to over communicate. Loop your teams in! You need them! They will make or break your success. You want them to love coming to work so much that they will give you their all and then some. If you are a jerk and sit there like a bump on a log, never informing them of happenings – *IT.WILL.BITE.YOU.IN.THE.ASS!*

Newbie Leader Pitfall #2: Ball Hogging It
Overview: Tell me that you know what a ball hog is! Consider the athlete who takes the shot over and over again—many times missing as well as not noticing that a teammate has a better shot and is not being guarded. In a business sense, these leaders either temporarily or permanently forget that they are not a one-monkey circus. They are leaders who are either oblivious to other very capable parties that have the ability to take over a portion (or all) of a task or simply a leader who is trying to do too much. Whatever the motivator, this pitfall is dangerous! There is no way one person can do everything. Were modern-day skyscrapers put together piece by piece by one single person? Hell, to the NO! If you choose to ball-hog tasks, projects, meetings, decisions, and so on, you may encounter the "live by the sword, die by the sword" if things go awry. This is also a very dangerous slippery slope as these leaders are likely not soliciting feedback from the players who are involved in the tasks. We sometimes see this when a leader makes a presentation on a process that he or she may oversee but not actually perform and not fully understand. In this scenario, a strong leader will call upon

the "experts" for input as well as spread the wealth in terms of involvement. At the end of the day, humans like to be included, we like to feel valued, and if you are not giving people a chance at providing input, they may not give you respect.

Risk: The major risk with ball hogging is simply alienating the staff, your colleagues, as well as the administration. You also risk loss of respect and notice a diminished effort among staff as well as overall poor employee morale.

Overcoming: Ask for input! Spread the wealth! Delegate, delegate, and …. DELEGATE! As a strong leader, you honestly want and need input from others. Besides risking the burnout factor of your own personal health, you are committing a major NO-NO by trying to do it all.

Newbie Leader Pitfall #3: The Blame Game
Overview: This occurs when a leader passes the blame for mistakes or failure on a task or project in lieu of taking ownership of the issue. The blame-game phenomenon goes beyond holding staff accountable but rather features throwing team members under the bus when shit hits the fan. Leaders are not the only professionals who can find themselves blaming others for failure. The blame game is not isolated to the work environment as people sometimes do this in their personal lives. Oddly enough, people sometimes start to believe the "blame" and lessen their feeling that they are personally responsible for the issue.

Risk: If you have not noticed, a common risk for these pitfalls continues throughout this chapter—staff resentment and alienation. As you can imagine, if a team turns their back to a leader or dreads working for a leader, the resulting diminished performance of the team can be detrimental to operations. When the overall morale of the team or individuals on the team becomes degraded, it can be very difficult to rebound.

Overcoming: The best way to overcome unnecessary blaming of others is to take ownership of one's mistakes. While this can be difficult at times, passing the buck often results in a rolling snowball of issues as it relates to perception of others. My husband and I are constantly reiterating to our children to own their mistakes. Taking responsibility is no different than a little child shamelessly admitting he or she took the cookie without asking, as opposed to blaming a sibling. I know I am simplifying here, but do not be afraid to hold yourself accountable. Likewise, be sure to look for signs of your team members or colleagues continuously playing the blame game. It is important to identify and coach team members on the importance of owning their actions.

Newbie Leader Pitfall #4: Avoidance of Conflict

Overview: While not always the case, new leaders can often find themselves a bit nervous when it comes to dealing with not-so-pleasant situations. This can be action items such as disciplining an employee, counseling an employee on an issue, serving as a moderator in a tense situation, and sometimes even letting employees go. There are opportunities for conflict and hurt feelings in those situations. Leaders encounter some not-so-fun interactions, and sometimes the gut feeling is to avoid the situation and hope it goes away. Avoiding an issue can be a recipe for disaster. Sometimes, avoiding a conflict can add an intense amount of fuel and introduce barriers that you may never expect. By avoiding, you are also not addressing opportunities for constructive feedback. It can be difficult, but new leaders need to find it from within to jump right into the uncomfortable situation and keep a positive attitude. One important thing to remember is that you will not always keep everyone happy. Quite frankly, people can become pissed off at some of the craziest things. As a leader, you need to confront conflict as an attempt to resolution before additional conflict can bubble up. Do not delay or put off a potential conflict. Attack it!

Risk: Simply stating – conflict is many times unavoidable in the workplace. There are typically too many personalities and moving parts in the equation for conflict to never appear.

Overcoming: A strong leader can recognize a potential situation and intervene or take other actions to simmer things down. Understanding that leaving a situation alone might equal a greater situation is a huge step in the right direction to becoming a successful leader.

Newbie Leader Pitfall #5: Too Hands-Off

Overview: A leader who is not being ingrained in the details of how to actually accomplish the tasks of his or her team can be very detrimental. This can result in underestimating what it takes as far as labor, time, and costs to accomplish day-to-day operations. When a leader cannot speak to the workflow within his or her span of control and scope, he or she often comes across in a negative light to peers who are seeking assistance or working through issues on behalf of other departments.

Risk: New leaders risk not absorbing information or understanding if they do not jump into the tasks at hand. There is typically no better way to learn than doing something yourself. When you take action and get involved, you have a better appreciation for how things work and can speak appropriately and intelligently about the area you oversee.

Overcoming: Do not be too proud to "take a ride along" with staff members or colleagues. If you do not understand something, do not be afraid to ask questions or ask for a demo. Ask your teams for a list of concerns or items that could help them do their job. By soliciting feedback, new leaders get the tried-and-true inside scoop from the people who are handling the work. Leaders who come in and sit in their office are often scorned with a loss of respect by their team. However, jumping right in and taking interest in what the team is doing and has to say can be a tremendous employee morale boost.

While we reviewed a small sampling of pitfalls that new leaders may experience, it is safe to say that there are many more hurdles that green leaders may encounter. It is also important to not only focus on the pitfalls but also the acceleration factors of success among new leaders. By focusing on the holistic picture, new leaders can obtain a better understanding of who they are and what they have to offer. In future editions, we will review additional pitfalls that new leaders may encounter.

ENHANCE

Chapter 7

• • •

DIG, MEN, DIG!

Landing your first big role is fantastic—a few high fives from your friends, maybe some hugs and celebratory dinners with your family, and just a whole lot of happiness going on. Although you will likely maintain that level of excitement for quite some time, how do you channel those emotions into buckling down and getting to work on a mission to be majorly successful? There is no easy answer to that one. Of course you find yourself absorbing all you can during your training program. You may notice that people in your area may look at you with a tilted head until they get to know your true potential. Again, age discrimination is absolutely not tolerated; however, perceptions can foster and hide various feelings.

The best way to become a trusted member of a team is to be dedicated. Be a resource that can be counted on. During the initial phase of your career, you need to focus on displaying that you truly do have the attitude to go the extra mile. This doesn't always mean that you need to be the first in the office and the last one out; however, that can be one way a younger professional shows his or her level of dedication.

Sometimes, gaining slivers of respect or tidbits of success is not glamorous. You are not always going to get a big pat on the back. Hell, to be honest, most of your efforts most of the time will go completely unnoticed. Or so you will think. Those that do get noticed are usually hidden as well. They can be conveyed in the behaviors of leaders, peers, or others after a job well done. They will be damned if they let YOU know that THEY are impressed, but sometimes you can pick up on nonverbal clues to ascertain this.

Despite this, you need to focus on the task at hand and NOT on the noise around the task. The most-sustained success is derived from little steps all layered upon one another in a strategic and methodical way. If you focus on menial tasks or the day-to-day burnout, you sometimes lose track of the bigger goal in mind—climbing your personal career ladder.

Close your eyes. What does your personal career ladder look like? How many rungs are acceptable to you? What measure marks the progression to the next rung? Does your ladder go straight up, or does it slowly lean to one focus or another? Do you have a safety net or fallback plan for your career ladder? This proverbial ladder is symbolic. It is something that YOU and only YOU must develop, manage, adjust, expand, enhance, revise, and build upon.

I can tell you that I had no clue that I was in charge of my own career ladder. I started my professional career with the mindset that the organization I was in would be mainly responsible for my career growth and that I was along for the ride. What I neglected to initially realize was that the people I worked for, the organization that I was a part of, my family/friends, and all external noise was just the environment that I was currently in.

In today's world, most people do not work for only one organization for their entire lives. They make various changes along the way. Sometimes, they take different roles in a current company; other times, they choose to leave and start a new career at a different company. Each change presents new challenges and opportunities. Nonetheless, the changes impact the person's career ladder.

Unfortunately, a major pitfall that newer professionals often neglect is the ability to see past the day-to-day grind. Yes, the project you are working on sucks ass, and it is fraught with frustration. *However,* usually, your whole career is not hinging upon your success on this specific project. Of course, each project and task will collectively add up to your reputation to deliver premier success, but getting too caught up in certain tasks can be devastating.

When you are slightly failing at something, it is without a doubt stressful. However, overcoming the situation and rendering all efforts to that recovery is such a beneficial practice. Think of that cliché about not being able to fully enjoy success without first experiencing failure.

This might sound so silly to you, but you truly NEED to fail from time to time. You gain important skills from handling difficult situations, being uncomfortable, being scolded, and quite honestly, just blowing the situation altogether. Now, I know many of you (myself included) get a shiver up and down the spine when you think about failing.

I am also certainly not saying to go out there and screw up situations so that you can dig yourself out of a hole. Hell, no! What I am saying is that we truly need to embrace finding ourselves in all sorts of situations. Let's look at an example of how you may feel when placed in two corporate conundrums—one positive and one negative. These scenarios are rather vague, but the overall goal of this activity is to ask you to consider the difference between succeeding and failing at a temporary level. Although continually failing—or succeeding, for that matter—can begin to affect a person's sense of well-being, there is benefit in breaking down and failing miserably.

Consider these two scenarios:

IF YOU…	HOW YOU FEEL…
Successfully led a project that met all deadlines and required outcomes	*WOO-HOO! I nailed that. I had no doubt I would rock that! I knew I would blow your socks off. Look how good I am. I feel fan-freak-ing-tastic!*
Totally forgot about a task that your boss asked you to do—she stressed that it was very important and gave you a deadline	*OMG, did I honestly forget to do that? She specifically told me that this was of utmost importance, and I blew it. I don't think she will ever count on me again.*

Now look at those two examples one more time. Which of the two do you think presents truly meaningful and valuable learning opportunities? In the first example, sure, you nailed it, but you may also begin to feel a bit invincible. You have emerging confidence that is peaking and growing. You know you can be counted on, and you may let your guard down. In the second example, you missed the mark. This can happen from time to time, and it isn't always a reason to be alarmed. Of course, we never want to fail or find ourselves in an unfortunate situation, but recovering from the situation is imperative. By recovering, we quickly show ourselves that the stressors we may have experienced do not define who we are as professionals. If you have a long-tenured career, you will for certain have ups and downs along the way. A good leader will recall upon both the negative and positive experiences when determining actions. Speaking of positives and negatives, think about your personal attributes – who the hell do you think you are?!? Follow me… let's dig into this and find out just WHO exactly you are!

EMBRACE

Chapter 8

* * *

WHO DO YOU THINK YOU ARE?

Have you ever wondered why some people are successful and others are not? Do you think success is a by-product of an action such as the school you attended or the environment in which you were raised? Well, the long and short answer to the burning question of success is that there is no single factor that preps younger professionals for success. There are so many instances of colleagues attending the same program and learning the same tools and material at the same school, yet they find that their paths are vastly different. Perhaps one career is launching at speeds greater than expectation and another is stalled looking for an opportunity to leave the gate toward. More than likely, the difference is not in the path that the colleagues took but rather in the people themselves.

Meet Bobby and Tommy. Bobby and Tommy attended the same university and studied the same engineering major. Yay – both Bobby and Tommy also graduated with honors from their

program. The guys vowed to stay in touch and continue to con-
nect on all things engineering as they launched their careers.
Bobby was diligent in his career planning. By the time he got his
diploma in his hot little hands, he was ready and cued up to hit
Submit on his application for junior engineer with a prestigious
engineering company. Sure, it wasn't his ideal job, but it was
a great place to start with a great company. Bobby landed the
position and was well into the role when he decided to reach out
to Tommy after a few months on the job. Tommy, on the other
hand, had no clue where to start. He spent his days after graduation looking around for leads on position, and his nights were
spent socializing. Because he had not yet found that PERFECT
position, he was reluctant to put his name in the hat for any position. He thought, *Hell, why not set my aspirations high?* Weeks
and weeks passed, and the two finally connected to discuss their
new lives and careers. Boy, what a shocker for Tommy to learn
that after six weeks, Bobby had already been promoted.

A scenario such as the above often results in one professional
zipping through a series of interpersonal questions: What's his
or her secret? Is he or she smarter than me? Why can't I land
a great role like him/her? Is he or she a better person than me?
Most likely, the answer to all of these questions is *no.* It is more
than likely that Bobby has learned how to harness his personal
power along with how to capitalize on his diligent and methodical career planning and focus. He has learned how to help shape
his path, accomplish his initial goals, and begin to realize his
potential.

Motivation—why can't I get motivated? Sadly, many younger adults and adults as well struggle with the lack of urgency to self-motivate and gain momentum. Likely, personal and professional stressors as well as external forces play a role in holding us back at times. Procrastination is a true motivation killer. While the thought process is there to kick it into gear, the desire to do something else can sometimes prevail and totally derail the task.

While it is not exactly known why some people generally possess more motivation than others, we know that various factors play into this. Many of us have heard stories about people who were at the top of their class with so much potential, yet somehow they never achieve success. Why does this occur? On the flip side, there are some who barely get through their academic lives only to become brilliant in their chosen fields. Ultimately, our upbringing, our education, our family and social ties, and many other influences all play a role in our success. However, when it comes down to it, YOU are responsible for your success or failure in both a personal and professional sense. You may find yourself like Bobby in our story above and soaring through your immediate goals, or you may find that you are treading water like Tommy. Either way, you are likely still moving forward each day.

While it may be easy to do, it is important to not place too much focus on comparing yourself to your peers. Sure, you may think that your paths should be aligned or similar, but chances are, they are vastly different. Likewise, your personal attributes, including traits such as motivation, dedication, and drive, all come into play with your ability to harness a successful path. Again, because we are all the captains of our own ships, our rate of success should be measured against the personal goals that we set forth along with where we see our career path aligning. This is really why you see such a discrepancy of professional success and failure between two very similar-appearing colleagues.

One of the main goals that Early Bird Executive has set out to accomplish is to help young professionals to embrace opportunity and develop a strong desire to achieve accelerated levels of success. At times, the notion that success is anywhere close on the radar can be felt. This is true especially of new professionals in the roller coaster of being a new leader. Many times, we find ourselves walking down the wrong road in our journey, and it takes stopping to think and ultimately recognize that the road is very far from our desired path. We may even not understand how we got there and feel a bit stuck. What if you were able to exit that road and begin to see the correct positive path form before your eyes? Would you run or walk to gain momentum?

What would your life look like if you knew that you couldn't fail? Consider yourself in a leadership role. What if you knew that whatever decision you took, failure was not a possibility? Would you take more risks? Would you try something that you have been wanting to put into action but have not had the balls to do it? Consider this type of mentality as an interruption to a bit of cowardice management style where professionals are so worried about failing that they never take chances. What differences can you see?

I think young professionals are poised to shake things up a bit. Sure, you may fail. However, what if some of the great innovators of our time did not shake things up a bit in their world? Would we have social media today? What about text messaging? Hell, would you have even been able to purchase this book with your computer on a website like Amazon if someone somewhere did not think, *Hell, why the hell not?*

WHO ARE YOU?

Do you like the person you are today? Would you have a beer with you if you just met you? Do you think that you have a positive attitude, or are you often filled with doubt and questioning? Our concept of ourselves can be our best trait or literally our worst. There are so many studies about how people feel about themselves and the impact on their personality and well-being. I am such a strong believer in thinking positively is part of the recipe for success. When you are confident, you enter into situations with a powerful sense of positive vibes.

WHAT ARE YOUR GOALS?

Goals truly serve as your road map in both your professional and personal life. Typical examples of personal goals are to get married, purchase a home, have children, and so forth. These are the type of thoughts and desires that you have likely been building as targets in your head for how you will live your life.

Professional goals often revolve around educational desires, industry aspirations, logistical requirements, and so forth—all items you desire to accomplish from a career perspective. By setting goals, we are determining an objective target for success. You have likely heard of the SMART acronym as it pertains to goals. With this, goals should always be subjective, measurable, realistic, and achieved in a specific time. It is one thing to set a goal, but the real focus is actually achieving, surpassing, and altering if needed. Younger professionals need to be prepared to monitor progress against their goals on a very regular basis. This step is particularly important so that goals can be adjusted or redefined as career desires change.

DO YOU TALK TO YOURSELF?

You should. Having regular conversations with yourself may sound silly, but there is nothing better than sitting in a quiet room and letting your inner self "talk." This is time for thinking through scenarios, determining actions, and most importantly, considering your next steps. Be careful not to talk too much! Sometimes your inner self wants to have life moving conversations at 2 AM when you are trying to sleep. There is a great time for self-talk and a time that is disruptive and can foster anxiety. Continuously reviewing the same items over and over in your head can add confusion and turn a simple decision or topic into the most complex puzzle ever. It is OK to "tell" yourself to call it a night – politely of course! This reminds me of something one of my favorite childhood friends and I had to do. We develop something called "beep". Basically, when the night got too late and we kept chatting away, one of us would say beep as a queue to the other to stop talking. I can't promise that the beeps always worked initially but after a while we did call it a night. If we didn't tell ourselves to put a lid on it, we would have NEVER stopped jabbering! It's OK to "beep" yourself!

WHO DO OTHERS THINK YOU ARE?

It is without a doubt that our reputation is one of the most sacred things we have. I have seen professionals (both newer and seasoned) crumple up their reputation and throw it into the trash. In the tight niches we often find our careers falling into, you are undoubtedly going to run into someone again at a later point *or* come in contact with someone who knows someone with whom you worked at one point. In my small world of health information management, this could not be truer. I have heard others talk about the bridges past colleagues have burned and the emphatic – "I WILL NEVER work with that person again." You truly never know when or where, or in what capacity you will encounter a person. Hell, I once interviewed a person for a regional vice-president role who happened to be the same person I once worked for in entry-level position years ago. What if the candidate had treated me poorly? Do you honestly think he or she would have been granted an interview? Our names are our trademarks. People remember if we were always late to work, if we treated others poorly and even sometimes if our work was good or bad. Always assume you are leaving a lasting impression—positive or negative—with someone. Hold that impression to your heart and be gosh-darn sure that the impression you leave is the one you want.

YOU WANT TO KNOW WHAT YOU DON'T KNOW!

It is great that you have the drive and desire to push your career to infinite heights! But GUESS WHAT? You have a lot to learn! We all do! As humans, we never stop learning. Do not be afraid of what you don't know—this is fuel for you to pursue. If you have a burning desire to understand the ins and outs of the supply chain, jump right in. Younger professionals are particularly adaptable, and it is OK to not know everything. If you are ever placed in a situation that you truly do not know the answer to, it is quite OK to say that you are not sure, and you will need to get back to them with the answer. This task-retrieval process is vital to the learning experience. You will quickly become proficient in where to find answers and the best way to do so. It is important to never be ashamed if you are lacking in knowledge in certain areas. To become the most-well-rounded professional, you should view these challenges as learning opportunities. Hell, you should even seek out these opportunities. Challenge yourself to understand topics that are very foreign to you. By sheer nature, learning is quickly contagious, and more than likely, you will find yourself moving quickly through topics.

The question of the day is not who does your boss, your friend, your family member, your lover, and so on, think you are; rather, it is *WHO DO YOU THINK YOU ARE?* That statement sounds a bit confrontational, but I can promise you that it truly is a call to understand all that you have become, where you can go, and how can you grow. Speaking of growing, let's talk about scaling this sucker all the way to the sky!

GROW

Chapter 9

• • •

CLIMB AS HIGH AS THE SKY!

Younger professionals are often extremely attentive to the needs of the business—at least those who want to accelerate their careers. To jump on the proverbial "fast track" to greater leadership responsibility, you need to think about the bigger picture at hand. This may come in the form of the broader scope of a project. Don't just review the project plan with blinders on. Make sure you are truly thinking as you look for unidentified risks, missing tasks, potential barriers, and other factors not clearly stated.

These low-hanging fruits are sometimes very easy to pull down, but they do require good analytical sense. Although you may not always be a savior when and if you find items that others missed, you may identify something important by reviewing intently with a fresh take on the process. The most important concept to keep in mind here is *DO NOT BE AFRAID TO SPEAK UP*! Let me say this another time but in a slightly different way: you owe it to yourself and your career to BRING ideas to the table. In the quest for accelerating your career, if you are not doing this and are merely sitting idle in meetings, for example, you will likely not enjoy the fast-tracking that you so desire.

Being a productive member of the team helps others to see the potential in your ability. We talked about this a few chapters ago—respect is something that all professionals need to gain before achieving greater things. Younger professionals need to start swaying the respect factor to their side fairly rapidly.

I cannot tell you how many times (and this still happens today, and I am thirty-three) I have walked into a boardroom or met with new people for the first time and they did a double take when I shook their hands. Perhaps they were expecting someone who appeared older because they initially equated that with "more qualified"? Well, I can tell you that those are my favorite situations!

Sure, they may start off a bit awkward, but maintaining a confident composure and focused demeanor is *KEY*! You know what you bring to the table, you know that you know your shit, and most importantly, you know that you are going to knock their socks off! There is nothing better than to progress through the meeting like a champion and nearly physically see the respect level rising in the interactions toward you.

At the end of the meeting, you want them thinking that the pleasure of the conversation is all on their side of the table; you want them to be in awe of your ability to be so effective in the meeting. Talk about a 180-degree turnaround! After a fast forward of about thirty minutes or so, you literally go from people thinking "Who's this kid? to *Why did we not know we had such an impressive professional on our team? We need to work with this person on many other issues we are having.*

The reason I rate that type of interaction at the top is because I think that overcoming such an intense level of stereotyping only happens when young professionals truly have the knowledge and effective demeanor to be a force to be reckoned with! The greater the WOW factor, the more you prove that you aren't just some "kid" and that you are just as capable, if not more so, than a colleague who has been in a similar role for dozens of years.

Another beautiful thing about the WOWZA factor here is that it helps to educate those holding preconceptions that judging someone based on appearance is not a good practice at all. Now, am I naïve to think that those doing the judging will change this practice? Heck, no! For at that moment when the respect factor is exploding off the charts, you have proven that being young does not necessitate being unseasoned.

I remember a time when I was working on a project in New York City, and a customer asked about my experience. Of course I was happy to oblige, and I provided him with a backdrop on my background. Upon my completion, he quickly smiled and said something to the effects of, "Dang! What were you, like, ten when you started in the field?" This is another minor incidence of indirect age discrimination in full force!

I laughed it off during the meeting, but later I thought about the interaction. After my analysis, I determined that upon meeting me, he was slightly taken back by my younger appearance. I will say that he did wait a bit after our introduction before asking about my background (about four hours or so). Either curiosity must have been weighing on him as he gained more and more respect as we worked together, *or* he had hoped his shock factor of correlating my physical appearance to what was coming out of my brain would subside. Either way, at the end of the interaction, I took his comment as a positive one—yes, maybe a tad demeaning in some ways but positive because he felt my intense background was impressive for what he conceived as being someone very young.

When we focus our efforts on climbing up our personal career ladders, we sometimes begin to get a bit of tunnel vision. Although being laser-focused on our goals is SUPER important, we really need to stop, think, and reevaluate our ladder structures quite often. Sometimes, we are pushed by external figures in one direction, and sometimes actions can cause us to think we need to slide up a rung, down a rung, or just a little sideways. Keep in mind that this is YOUR career path, not someone else's! You own the destiny in many ways, based on the choices and strategic moves you make.

I hate to be a downer, but consider that a person who is pushing you in a certain direction MAY *not* always have your best interest in mind. This can come from many different avenues. Take for example a direct manager dramatically pushing you to transfer to a new role. Depending on the "spin" this manager puts on his or her pitch, you may or may not be able to read between the lines. Perhaps your manager knows that your position is being eliminated, but he or she is not able to tell you about this change. However, if the manager knows that you are a strong asset to the company, he or she may be using this tactic to keep you with the company.

Conversely, if you encounter a colleague who is repeatedly sending you job openings, there may be reason to think that the practice is not so innocent. Sure, you can confront the colleague by questioning why he or she is sending you new opportunities, but you may not get a truthful answer. The colleague may reply with the standard "Oh, I thought it might be something you were interested in."

Hmm, that's funny. I am not looking for another position. If you start to drill down that path, you may learn that the colleague is potentially purposely trying to get rid of you for his or her own personal gain. Maybe you are shining too brightly for that colleague. Well, guess what? Keep shining as bright as you can. *YOU* are the one who decides your career path!

Yeah, yeah, I know those two examples are only a few scenarios, and I made them pretty vague and predictable. However, there is a method to my madness! The point is that you may *never* fully understand the motives of other people; business decisions in general, market-driving factors, and several other variables. Because of this, the best focus you can put on your career growth is in the planning and thought progression that comes out of your own brain—yep, the old gray matter. I think it is pretty safe to say that all of us trust ourselves quite a bit.

I don't remember the last time I thought my brain was lying to me. I can be fair and say that I may still overanalyze some thoughts that come out of my brain, but it is pretty damn solid as far as leading me down the right path. First comes your brain, then comes your emotional thoughts on a decision. Those two interactions, along with a small quorum of folks (spouse, family members, friends), are really all you need to help keep that career ladder thriving and building.

Please be sure to NEVER underestimate the spouse/family/friend input factor. This support system is absolutely vital to helping you along the way. Do not assume that they will provide guidance one way or the other—let the advice flow. This emphasis also does not mean that you must always take their opinions and input as the right answers. However, be sure to listen to what they are telling you. Try your best to break down the words that they are speaking to you. Sometimes—and I am certainly guilty of this—we block out (inadvertently or intentionally) certain scenarios or possibilities.

To me, my husband is famous for giving input like this. He really plays the what-ifs with me, and sometimes I cannot stand him for it! However, I have definitely learned to start giving his thoughts more consideration because he has been right a bunch more times than I care to admit. (*Crap! I hope he doesn't read this book Oh, who am I kidding? Hi, Adam!*) In all seriousness, I have learned to really love the what-ifs and possibilities questions.

This is also very true in business. Sometimes people apologize about asking so many questions or asking for my clarification. I quickly jump in by noting that their questions are vital! Sometimes, their questions or inquiries help to identify things that I or others have not thought of. To me, this is what a strong team does. This is also what you need to do as a young professional.

We talked about this in the project plan example a bit ago—don't be afraid to question the heck out of something! Your thought or question may help avoid a disaster, or perhaps even save the company thousands of dollars. You would feel pretty crummy if an incident occurred, the team reviewed it on a status call, and you thought to yourself, *hmmn, I remember wondering if that test was necessary, but I didn't have the balls to ask because I assumed that someone else would have caught it if it was.* If that happens to you, it means that you aren't contributing as much as a high performer would. You want to be on the cutting edge of contributing. Of course, you don't want to come across as annoying, condescending, or demeaning, and we will talk in future books in this series about how to avoid that. It is a balancing act, to be sure. Be a gymnast. Jump on the beam and fine-tune that concept!

REVIEW

Chapter 10

* * *

TO SUM IT UP...

The truth of the matter is that scaling up your career ladder at lightning speed does NOT always equate to soaring salaries. However, if you make strategic and well-planned moves, you will see the amounts of money that you are offered begin to climb higher and higher. Another thing that you must be careful to avoid is making too many moves too fast. A résumé with many short-term engagements can be a red flag. Potential employers might begin to think that you have problems maintaining a level of longevity in any given role. In my experience, it is best to allow each role to run its course in terms of what you are learning and attaining from it. When you begin to feel less challenged and are noticing that your responsibilities are becoming many of the same, it may be a sign that you need to seek a more challenging role. Before making such moves, it is important to be sure to always maintain your reputation. You honestly never know when/where/how you will encounter a colleague or boss from the past. In a later volume in the Early Bird Executives Presents series, we spend the entire book discussing reputation—how to develop a good one, how to enhance it, and most importantly, how to ensure that it NEVER degrades.

One of the most important mind-sets that young professionals must ensure they have is that career growth can be accelerated in their twenties and thirties, with the goal that they will see their responsibilities and salaries skyrocket. It is by no means easy to overcome the stereotyping, prejudice, and lack of respect that younger professionals sometimes must endure. However, by overcoming these obstacles and handling them with grace, you become a stronger person and a better-equipped leader.

I am not going to lie—to some extent, I can understand some of the prejudicial behavior exhibited. There are some areas in which more seasoned individuals may have the upper hand. I also think that some of the questionable behavior stems from the people's own insecurities. They may be questioning their ability to "compete" with someone who may have stronger technology skills or other skills that transition with the various waves of changing tools. Heck, they may also flat out be jealous that you are in your role, and they were *way* back when they were your age. Regardless of the reason, it can be quite clear that some people are going to be bigger pains in the ass than others.

I know that I have emphasized the personal career ladder throughout this book. One of the areas that I continually place focus on in my own mind is that of goal setting. I remember telling my husband that I wanted to make $100,000 a year by the time I turned thirty. Putting this goal into motion allowed me to further plan and then determine what moves I needed to make. I can tell you that I have easily beat my goal, and I am still climbing stronger, well above that goal, as I sit here at age thirty-three. I do have other goals for other age milestones, and those are being honed in on more and more as time rolls on.

I would ask that each of you now take out the earlier exercise that you so hated but were obliged to complete because you were ever so politely asked. What do you see on that piece of paper covered in methodical ideas? Do you see freedom? Do you see a lot of work? Were you as aggressive as you would have liked, or maybe a bit too aggressive? Where do you see yourself in...

Six months?

Twelve months?

Two years?

Five years?

And beyond?

Obviously, none of us are psychic, and we certainly cannot define the future. Hell, our goals may fall flat, or we might encounter some tremendous roadblocks that require us to drastically change our goals. To be honest, those things are all fine. The most important thing is to continue to revise, erase, write, and review. The cycle of review is not black and white, but it does involve effort. Setting it and forgetting it—like they do in the infomercials—will not get you to career success.

Don't forget to rely on your trusted support system. These people can prove so valuable if you are forced to perform the erasing and revising steps. They can help you define and plan for your next endeavor. They should also be a great support net so that when you are feeling discouraged, they can help brush the dust off you and pull you to your feet. I hate to say *tunnel vision* here because that isn't usually thought of as a good thing; however, if you think of a long freight train tunnel and can see that light at the end, each chug forward gets you closer and closer. Some trains move faster than others, and sometimes trains can move way too fast. You control your train and each chug forward.

Do you feel a bit more equipped to lead that train safely to your goal? My hope is that this series will give you some good career-advancement advice centered on those of you who are younger and are fast-tracking your careers. You are definitely not alone. There are publications that routinely award the top "thirty under thirty," or things to that effect. Hell, I just saw a press conference on a professional sports team hiring a general manager who was a cool thirty-one years old. When they began to highlight his experience to date, it was quite impressive to see that he had made such a positive impact on so many teams in his relatively brief career.

I think the cliché "Age is just a number" is a bit annoying. Of course, my whole premise is that younger professionals can make just as big of an impact as seasoned professionals can. However, that adage is overused. I do not think that it packs as good of a punch as it can. It is quite easy to say those words, but strong professionals do not waste their time thinking about that. Accelerating professionals jump right into firing out their ideas, recalling knowledge from their experience, and most importantly, PERFORMING!

I'm sure that many of you might have picked up this book not knowing what to expect. I want you to burn this thought deep within you as you find your roles growing and growing: be sure to always have at the top of your mind that you are in that position for a reason. There were certain powers that be who could truly see your potential and took a chance on you. You are now there to take things to the next level.

If we keep in mind the thought that we want our leaders to continually think *I am so happy I hired him/her*, then we see the need to keep challenging ourselves. As I have said, speak up—have the balls you need to be actively engaged. Never sit idle when you really have a contributing thought. Be sure to carry yourself with grace, self-respect, dignity, and a learning eye. And most importantly, be an innovator. Be disruptive. Don't just sit back and let things stay status quo. Ask yourself whether there is another way to accomplish the task at hand. If there is, don't be afraid to bring it to the table.

If you want to be successful, you need to think about the head of the table. What is it going to take to get to the head? I am quite sure that most of our great business leaders do not spend their time just sitting idle. There are plenty of idle people in business. To be honest, many of them are happy being idle.

They want to be able to go to work, do their job, and leave. They don't want to be leaders, they don't want to give more, and quite frankly, they typically cannot even be motivated to do more.

Something tells me that you are not one of those people because you are reading this book. You are choosing to focus on pushing your career. *YOU WANT MORE!* The funny thing is that you do not always need to work crazy hours, burn yourself out, and have no life. Hell, I've managed to have four children, an active social life, a husband, a dog, and a house to hold down while I have been growing my career.

There are perks to wanting it ALL like I did. That is, I decided that I wanted it all—a family and a career—and I built my career ladder to sustain this. I cannot tell you how many times I have encountered people who have focused on one or the other and regret that choice. Of course, if you only want a career and no children, that is awesome—you have defined your life path. If you have decided you want children and no career, more power to you (I doubt you are reading this book, but hell, I'll give you kudos, too).

Career growth is a complicated yet very dynamic and fluid process. You are human. You cannot prepare for or possibly prevent or even make happen every single little variation of your plan. To mitigate this, you need to keep an open mind. While going down your path, remember that your journey is full of analyses, learning experiences, failures, successes, and some stressful times. Be sure to adjust and build upon your career path and where you ultimately want to go. Without that basic framework, you are dead in the water. It is easy to get caught up in the hectic day-to-day grind, but set aside some time to look at your strategy. You may even find that your strategy needs to be adjusted, which is totally fine.

Youthful leaders of today, let's rise! It is not a coincidence how Early Bird Executives got its name. It is true that the early achiever and arriver is there to get shit done. Let's help remove the prejudice and be extreme contributors in our roles. It's OK to shock and wow your colleagues; they will also learn from you, so be sure to make an impact. When you make an impact today, you are growing your later value. Most importantly, remember that you are qualified for the role, you are certainly ready for the challenge, and you are most definitely deserving of the salary and perks that come with such responsibilities. Anyone who tries to look down on you—essentially saying, "You're just a kid!" without actually saying it—can go screw themselves. You are definitely a force to be reckoned with. You are *YOU*, and gosh darn it; you have an amazing career ahead of you. *GO GET 'EM!*

Talk to you next time, my friends. Check out the other titles in the series on the last page of this book, as you will want to continue the conversation with me. Let's move over there!

Early Bird Executives Presents is a series that highlights the trials and tribulations of being a young adult in today's fast-paced business world.

The key focus is on empowering and educating today's younger workforce on how to jump-start the path to success, as told through the eyes of a thirty-something corporate executive who began her progressive management growth in her late teens. Overcoming varying levels of reverse age discrimination, earning the trust of very seasoned leaders, and all the steps along the way to success are reviewed. Many tips, thoughts, and guides enrich the reading and make for a very meaningful experience.

The contents go beyond landing the first leadership role and also put special focus on growing, accelerating, and maintaining the lead. This series is also useful for parents/families who have set high goals for their children's level of success. Through this series, parents/families can become better educated on how they can contribute to and encourage the fast track to success for their loved ones.

The series is full of humor, assertiveness, plenty of honesty and truthful career hacks that will catapult young adults to higher levels than they ever thought possible. Buckle up, give social media a break, and get ready to look at career development in a way you have never seen!

ABOUT THE AUTHOR

Shannon L. Baxa, MS, RHIA, PMP, has been a force to be reckoned with ever since she left the halls of her small-town high school. After a few months of exploring various options, she landed an entry-level file-clerk position that would totally change her life. Shannon used her time as a file clerk to be a complete sponge of all things business. Soon after developing her vision and goals, she set off on an exciting journey.

Throughout the Early Bird Executives series authored by Baxa, we learn of her methodical and precise moves that enabled her to quickly climb the corporate ladder. She has enjoyed watching her salary and responsibilities multiply many times over. Shannon has a true passion for mentoring and empowering others to take leaps they never imagined—this focused drive shines so bright in her writing. It's great to see how a young woman from a town of two hundred people and born to parents who took much different career paths is touching so many lives in her health-care leadership role and additional position as a college educator.

We invite you to jump on the Early Bird Executives rocket. You better buckle up. The launch is ready—are you?

OTHER TITLES IN THE EARLY BIRD EXECUTIVES PRESENTS SERIES

Early Bird Executives Presents…
Your Future Starts Now!

Early Bird Executives Presents…
Guide to Choosing a Career You *LOVE*

Early Bird Executives Presents…
Guide to WOWing Everyone You Meet

Early Bird Executives Presents…
Guide to Establishing a Stellar Reputation

Early Bird Executives Presents…
Guide to Career Growth and Sustainability

Find more resources, personalized mentoring services, as well as tools, articles, and blogs at

www.EarlyBirdExecutives.com

"Like" us on Facebook:

www.facebook.com/EarlyBirdExecutives.com

www.ingramcontent.com/pod-product-compliance
Lightning Source LLC
Chambersburg PA
CBHW021411170526
45164CB00002B/597